"It's not about having a philosophy.
It's about adapting to the quality of the
opposition."

– Jurgen Klopp

Business Readiness Levels
By Richie Ramsden and Mo Chowdhury

First edition 2019
This edition (3rd) 2019

ISBN: 9781082195723

Independently published

The Business Readiness Levels

The Simple Benchmark for Business Ventures

Richie Ramsden and Mo Chowdhury

Contents

Executive Summary

The Business Readiness Levels (BRL) are a way to benchmark the current status of a venture - from concept to mature business.

The BRL help to identify the level of maturity of a business venture, or innovation project.

They allow a user to:

- Manage the blend of skills in a venture
- Show progress and plan for next steps
- Manage the risk for investments in ventures.

The BRL can also be a more formal way to identify when a project needs to pivot, change or be closed down.

The BRL are a complimentary system to the Technology Readiness Levels (TRL) often used to communicate research maturity.

Chapter One:
The Start

Establishing Benchmarks

The Technology Readiness Levels are often used to show the maturity of an innovation. A system to show the level of progress in a business venture is not as well established.

What are the Technology Readiness Levels?

The Technology Readiness Levels (TRL) are used by NASA, the European Space Agency and many other institutes to easily communicate the progress of a technical concept.

The TRL system is rated from TRL1 ("Basic principles") to TRL9 ("Technology concept operational in environment").

A version of the TRL can be seen below.

Technology Readiness Level	
1	Basic principles
2	Technology concept formulated
3	Proof of concept
4	Validated technical concept in laboratory
5	Validated technical concept in relevant environment
6	Technology concept demonstrated in relevant environment
7	Prototype demonstration in operational environment
8	Technology Concept qualified
9	Technology Concept operational in environment

The TRLs provides a universal method to benchmark the level of progression of a technical concept and allows technical teams to communicate effectively when discussing maturity levels.

The TRLs:

- Are a universal system to ensure that maturity level can be easily benchmarked
- Allow easy communication of progress when a concept is diagnosed over time
- Provide a structure to plan progress to the next level of maturity

Current examples of Technology Readiness Levels are shown below:

TRL 1-2:   Quantum Computers
TRL 4-6:   Blockchain
TRL 7-9:   GPS

Where do the BRL fit in?

The Business Readiness Levels compliment the TRL and cover a range from Concept (BRL1) to Fully Embedded Business (BRL9).

The advantages of a universal system of TRL apply also to the BRL - communication of maturity, progress and ease of planning.

The BRL is of particular use when developing a plan to mature a venture - providing a guide as to what to do to push a venture forward.

Chapter Two:
The Business Readiness Levels

What are the Levels?

The BRL are shown below, alongside questions which can be used to diagnose the maturity level.

	Business Readiness Level	Question
1	Concept	Is this a new idea?
2	Problem-solution fit	Why would someone want this?
3	Build team and plan	What do we need to start and how do we get it?
4	Customer definition	Who can we ask to check that people really want this?
5	Hypothesis testing	Will people pay for it?
6	Minimum viable product (MVP)	Is this product good enough for now?
7	Feedback loop	What do I do with the customer feedback?
8	Scale	What features should we add next?
9	Fully embedded business	Fully embedded business

Some things to note of progress:

- The cadence of reaching new levels of the BRL will vary in relation to the current level, and the venture itself

- Some ventures can rapidly progress through the first few levels in a sprint fashion. Later levels require external input and so will take longer to achieve

- The BRL are not designed to evenly break the venture maturity timeline into same-sized chunks, rather to establish a series of milestones in maturity

- Progress through the BRL can be non-linear. If a venture pivots (to a new customer segment or value opposition), it is good practice to return to earlier BRL to confirm the foundations

- Each venture should be regularly diagnosed and planned for individually. This includes ventures which have multiple value propositions or customer segments

The BRL in detail

The BRL of a venture can be determined with the characteristics shown in this section. These levels also include areas that should be considered a risk to the venture at each stage.

It should be noted that to progress to the next level with a venture, the characteristics of the next phase are to be considered. These should form the basis of a plan to proceed.

BRL1: Concept

Business Readiness Level 1 can be characterised as:
The first idea of a venture or an innovation.

- The Innovation could be well 'thought through'

- A customer, problem or solution may be apparent however they remain nebulous and cannot be well described

- This venture has been formed by one person, or discussed within a small group

- No plan of how to reduce business venture risk or where to take the innovation next can be demonstrated

A business in BRL1 will find funding or external emotional investment hard to acquire, due to the early stage of development.

Often at this stage it is considered that a great idea is enough to go to market.

BRL2: Problem-Solution Fit

Business Readiness Level 2 can be characterised as:
The problem has been identified and the proposed solution will address it.

- The solution can satisfy a customer pain, but can also be a customer gain that is not yet in place

- The solution has the potential to solve the high-level problem, or provide an untapped gain

- There is not already a solution in the market to the problem or untapped gain

- An idea of who might benefit from the idea is taking shape however a formalised Value Proposition Canvas is not yet ready

A business in BRL2 may tend to consider a potential solution as complete early on and move to build stage (MVP) without appropriate validation of problem and customer needs.

BRL3: Build Team and Plan

Business Readiness Level 3 can be characterised as:
The skills required are known and a team is formed.

- A map of the skills needed to explore the venture is developed

- The team should have access to the following skills or resources:
    - Market expertise in proposed area
    - Subject matter experts
    - Critical friends
    - Customers– this may be hard to secure at BRL3

- If potential customers are secured care must be taken to ensure that single customer bias does not occur

A business at **BRL3** may tend to arrange a team of like-minded individuals who see the solution and problem in the same way, including individual customers who have a strong problem to solve.

BRL4: Customer Definition

Business Readiness Level 4 can be characterised as: Customer segment is known and well defined, including customer characteristics.

- Formally, the customer pains and gains have been considered, and the potential solution adapted to satisfy requirements

- The desirability, feasibility and viability of the business venture can be demonstrated

- The Business Model Canvas (BMC) and Value Proposition Canvas (VPC) or similar documentation can be demonstrated.

A business at BRL4 may treat value proposition documentation and proposed business as a formality, but these should be regularly revised and challenged during the business venture development.

BRL5: Hypothesis Testing

Business Readiness Level 5 can be characterised as:
Having a list of hypotheses which can be tested.

- A formal plan is in place, and is executed to test hypothesise and assumptions

- Experiments should be carried out to test
  - Customer desirability
  - Market desirability
  - Solution/problem fit

- Experiments can also be carried out to verify viability and feasibility of the venture

- Results are recorded and evidence supporting business venture can be demonstrated

A business in BRL5 can be susceptible to evidence bias, placing great emphasis on low level evidence that supports the venture assumptions. The critical friend is crucial in this level, to challenge strength, volume and customer proximity of evidence.

BRL6: Minimum Viable Product

Business Readiness Level 6 can be characterised as:
Having released an MVP.

- A minimum viable product (MVP) is defined and constructed to provide the minimum features possible to deliver some value to the customer

- An MVP may be a service (Concierge or Wizard-of-Oz) or a product

- Early adopter customers are willing to purchase the solution in order to access value

A business in BRL6 may struggle to define the minimum criteria for an MVP. Care should be taken in this level not to engineer features of a value proposition which are not essential.

BRL7: Feedback Loop

Business Readiness Level 7 can be characterised as:
The feedback loop of features which are developed alongside early adopters and customers.

- Feedback from customers is regularly collected

- New solutions or new features are designed for the business venture

- A prioritised roadmap of features and future product management strategy is developed.

Businesses in BRL7 may risk building a product for a single customer or small group in the customer segment. The value proposition and business model must be revisited regularly in order to define a global list of priority features.

BRL8: Scale

Business Readiness Level 8 can be characterised as:
A product or service has been developed beyond an MVP stage.

- New customers are regularly acquired

- Demonstrated evidence of exploration into new or adjacent markets

- The roadmap and product strategy are embedded with new features to the offering being regularly introduced and value tested.

Businesses in BRL8 may be inclined to reduce energy in strategy/mapping of customer needs and related value-added features in favour of sales. In order to scale most effectively continuous testing of hypotheses of target market and new markets must be carried out.

BRL9: Fully Embedded Business

Business Readiness Level 9 can be characterised as:
A business model or venture that is fully embedded in a market (or many markets).

- The business has a healthy revenue stream, business development and formal future development and growth strategy

- Company is well known in market or industry

- Company may have lobbying capabilities

A company in **BRL9** may be at risk of disruption from adjacent markets new business models or new products.

Chapter Three:
Using the BRL

BRL and project management

In order to complete any project in a timely manner, there is a requirement to focus time, energy and resources in the right place. The BRL in combination with TRL, helps project managers to understand any imbalances between technical and business drive.

BRL vs TRL allows you to check where effort is needed - and address it quickly.

If the venture strays outside the 'well balanced innovation' zone, then more focus is needed on the aspect which will re-balance it - like a football team focusing on defence or attack in different phases of the game.

In simple terms, if the BRL and TRL are balanced within 2/3 levels or each other, then project skills and progress is considered well-balanced.

If this mismatch of levels stretches beyond 2/3 levels, then effort must be focused on re-balancing in the deficient skill area.

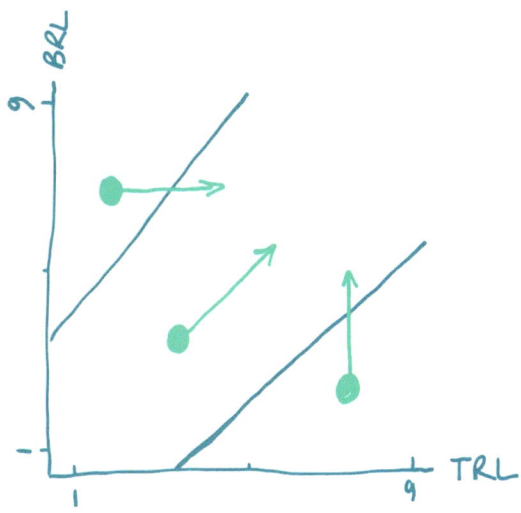

For example, if a project is well progressed in the BRL level at BRL5 but the TRL is low at TRL2, then more technical focus is needed.

Similarly, if a technology is well progressed at TRL7 but the venture BRL is at 2 focus must be rebalanced on business skills.

In this latter example, focus should be on pushing to BRL3 by forming an appropriate team to challenge the value proposition assumptions.

Case study 1

A highly developed technology targeted in another market

A company develops a web application which presents up-to-date status data to a customer in a dashboard.

An MVP has been delivered to market and is generating revenue from the data pipelines which are robust and are delivering data when needed to the customer as visuals.

This project is well balanced, with a BRL and TRL of 7.

Feedback is received from a potential customer that the data may also be useful if delivered to data analysts for use in their risk models or actuarial calculations.

The TRL remains at 7 - the data pipelines are still in service - however the change in customer and value proposition means the BRL for this concept is at BRL 2 – understanding problem solution fit.

Course of action

This team should put every effort into progress in the BRL to ensure that the venture is well balanced in both directions. This can be done rapidly, reaching MVP level quickly but they must focus on rebalancing the venture.

The risk of failure of a venture with well-developed technology, but an unclear idea of the customer, is as high as a venture with a clear idea of an MVP but with no technology to deliver it.

BRL and risk management

The level of risk is always high in an innovation or venture. Understanding what to do to minimise the inherent risk is vital in preventing problems.

The BRL system can be used to benchmark the current level of progress in the venture - and help in defining what action can be taken to reduce the inherent risk.

When collaborating or co-creating new value propositions with other companies or institutes, an assessment of BRL is as vital as the assessment of their technical advancement in the field.

For example: A company has a high maturity in TRL and BRL (7-9) in a field. In a new market however, the BRL may be significantly lower.

In the formation of a collaboration, joint development or co-creation agreement, the BRL must be progressed in order to minimise the uncertainty in the venture.

Case study 2

TechCo: A potential partner company in a new venture

TechCo contacts you with an idea for co-creation of an idea. The company has been established in their field for some time, however this new value proposition is in a new market and they need your expertise to execute it.

The BRL of *TechCo*'s current ventures is high (BRL9), and their TRL is also high (9).

The temptation could be to test the technology internally to ensure its compatibility, and then look for external trials with customers (BRL6).

This would have very high risk and may damage reputation and revenues.

Course of action

Begin at BRL1 and work through the levels. This may take a small amount of time, particularly if the new venture idea is already well formed, however it will assist greatly in managing the uncertainty and risk to both companies.

Case study 3

FreshLookTech: An investment

FreshLookTech an early-stage company comes to light which operates in a similar market to you but with new technology or a fresh-value proposition. Often start-ups act rapidly and as such *FreshLookTech* has only been trading for 1 year.

It is tempting to invest smaller amounts in start-up companies to have some stake in the disruption of your current market or ventures but how much and when should you invest?

Course of Action

Firstly look at their financials. Any investment or acquisition decision should be based on an understanding of their financials.

If there is currently no revenue and you are acting on potential business revenues in the future, the uncertainty/risk can be mitigated by diagnosing *FreshLookTech* against the BRL.

A company with a low BRL will hold higher

inherent risk as an investment than a company with a more advanced BRL.

A company with a low BRL will hold higher inherent risk as an investment than a company with a more advanced BRL.

This also gives *FreshLookTech* some structure to work with to provide evidence to minimise uncertainty for your investment

Chapter Four:
The End

Conclusion

The Business Readiness Levels have the potential to help communicate the maturity of ventures across many disciplines.

Project managers can use it to demonstrate progress and balance skills make-up when used with the technology readiness level.

When analysing new start-ups or venture from outside a company the BRL can be used to understand the current risk level as well as the progress needed to reach an appropriate level.

There will be many more uses for the Business Readiness Levels in other disciplines and many more will be explored as the concept evolves.

The Authors

The Authors

Richie Ramsden has many years' experience in leading technical and business projects. He started life as a polymer chemist, carrying out fundamental lab-based research before making the transition to project management, and data science.

Richie thinks digital technology can help resolve real problems, but always with people at the centre.

Richie also holds several patents in the application of large data-sets in predicting product performance.

Richie is also a Fellow of the National Innovation Centre for Data.

Mo Chowdhury is passionate about developing the next generation of products and services from transformative innovation. His background in Chemistry combined with his avid interest in digital technology & disruption plays a vital role in appreciating the balance of technical requirements whilst developing a business venture.

Mo has a strong focus on harnessing the power of external collaboration for project development. Previous successes have been realised but not limited to engaging with, start-ups and SMEs, government bodies and academia.